W9-AHI-030

The First Family of
HOPE

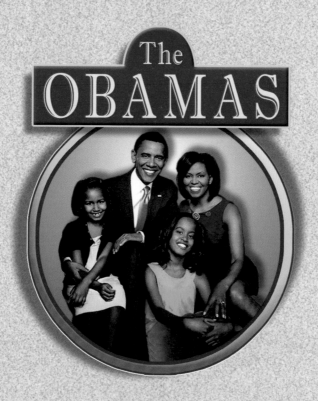

The OBAMAS

Barack
Michelle
Malia
Sasha
The Obama Family Tree
Obama Mania

Malia

Gail Snyder

Mason Crest Publishers

Produced by 21st Century Publishing and Communications, Inc.

MASON CREST PUBLISHERS INC.
370 Reed Road
Broomall, Pennsylvania 19008
(866) MCP-BOOK (toll free)
www.masoncrest.com

Printed in the United States of America.

First Printing

9 8 7 6 5 4 3 2 1

Library of Congress Cataloging-in-Publication Data applied for.

Snyder, Gail.
  Malia / Gail Snyder.
    p. cm.—(The Obamas : first family of hope)
  ISBN 978-1-4222-1479-4 (hardcover : alk. paper)
  ISBN 978-1-4222-1486-2 (pbk. : alk. paper)
  1. Obama, Malia, 1998–   —Juvenile literature. 2. Obama, Malia,
1998–   —Family—Juvenile literature. 3. Children of presidents—United
States—Biography—Juvenile literature. 4. Daughters—United States—
Biography—Juvenile literature. 5. Obama, Barack—Juvenile literature.
I. Title.
E909.O23S64 2009
973.932092—dc22
[B]   2009000167

Publisher's notes:
All quotations in this book come from original sources, and contain the spelling
and grammatical inconsistencies of the original text.

The Web sites mentioned in this book were active at the time of publication.
The publisher is not responsible for Web sites that have changed their addresses
or discontinued operation since the date of publication. The publisher will
review and update the Web site addresses each time the book is reprinted.

Contents

Introduction

On November 4, 2008, Barack Obama made history—he was the first black American to be elected president of the United States. The Obama family—Barack, wife Michelle, and daughters Malia and Sasha, became the first African-American first family.

THE FIRST FAMILY OF HOPE

The stories of the Obamas are fascinating and uniquely American. The six books in this series take you center stage and behind the scenes, with crafted and insightful storytelling, as well as hundreds of dynamic and telling photographs. Discover six unique inside perspectives on the Obama family's extraordinary journey and the Obama mania that surrounds it.

WHERE IT ALL BEGAN

Many generations ago, in the late 1600s, Barack's mother's ancestors arrived in colonial America as white emigrants from Europe, while his father's ancestors lived in villages in Kenya, Africa. Michelle's ancestors were shipped from Africa to America as slaves.

Generations later, Barack, son of a black father and a white mother, spent his childhood in Hawaii and Indonesia; while Michelle, a descendant of slaves, was growing up in Chicago. Later they both graduated from Harvard Law School, got married, and became proud parents of two beautiful daughters. Barack tackled injustice as a community organizer in Chicago, later entered politics, and was elected to the U.S. Senate.

"THE AUDACITY OF HOPE"

In 2004, at the Democratic National Convention, Barack Obama made an electrifying keynote speech, "The Audacity of Hope." He asked Americans to find unity in diversity and hope in the future. His message resonated with the attendees and millions of television viewers. Barack was catapulted from obscurity into the spotlight, and the Obama phenomenon had begun.

"YES WE CAN!"

On February 10, 2007, Barack announced his candidacy for the office of president of the United States. His family and legions of volunteers all over the country campaigned vigorously for him, and nearly two years later, the Obama family stood proudly in front of more than 240,000 supporters who gathered to hear Barack's victory speech. Tears streamed down the

The Obamas (left to right) Malia, Michelle, Sasha, and Barack, wave to their devoted fans. Barack has energized millions of people in the United States and around the world with his message of unity and hope.

faces of people who believed this was nothing short of a miracle. Tens of millions of television viewers worldwide watched and listened with a renewed sense of hope as President-elect Obama proclaimed:

> **❝ This victory is yours. . . . If there is anyone out there who still doubts that America is a place where all things are possible; who still wonders if the dream of our founders is alive in our time; who still questions the power of our democracy, tonight is your answer. ❞**

OBAMA FAMILY TIMELINE

1600s to 1700s
Barack Obama's mother's ancestors immigrate to the American colonies from Europe.

1936
Barack Obama, Sr., Barack's father, is born in a small village in Kenya, Africa.

1964
Barack's parents, Barack Obama, Sr. and Ann Dunham are divorced.

1700s to 1800s
Michelle Robinson Obama's ancestors arrive in the American colonies as slaves.

1937
Michelle's mother, Marian Shields, is born.

1967
Barack's mother marries Lolo Soetoro and moves the family to Soetoro's home country, Indonesia.

1850s
Michelle's great-great grandfather is born a slave in South Carolina.

1942
Barack's mother, Ann Dunham, is born in Kansas.

1971
Barack returns to Hawaii and lives with his grandparents.

1600   **1900**   **1950**   **1982**

1912
Michelle's grandfather, Fraser Robinson Jr., is born.

1959
Barack Obama, Sr. comes to America as a student.

1979
Barack graduates from high school and enrolls in Occidental College in Los Angeles, California.

1918
Barack's grandfather, Stanley Dunham, is born.

February 21, 1961
Barack Obama, Sr. and Ann Dunham are married.

1922
Barack's grandmother, Madelyn Payne, is born.

August 4, 1961
Barack is born in Honolulu, Hawaii.

1981
Barack transfers to Columbia University in New York City.

1935
Michelle's father, Fraser Robinson III, is born.

January 17, 1964
Michelle is born in Chicago, Illinois.

1982
Barack's father dies in Kenya, Africa.

1988

Michelle graduates from Harvard Law School.

1988

Barack enters Harvard Law School.

1990

Barack is elected president of the *Harvard Law Review*.

1991

Barack graduates from Harvard Law School.

1995

Barack's first book, *Dreams from My Father*, is published.

1998

Barack and Michelle's first daughter, Malia, is born.

2001

Barack and Michelle's second daughter, Sasha, is born.

July 2004

Barack delivers keynote speech at Democratic National Convention.

November 2, 2008

Barack's grandmother dies in Hawaii.

November 4, 2008

Barack is elected the first African-American president of the United States.

January 20, 2009

Barack is sworn in as the 44th president of the United States.

1983   1995   2006   2009

1988

Barack visits his relatives in Kenya, Africa.

1985

Michelle graduates from Princeton University.

1985

Barack moves to Chicago, Illinois, to work as a community organizer.

1983

Barack graduates from Columbia University.

1996

Barack is elected to the Illinois State Senate.

1995

Barack's mother dies.

1992

Barack and Michelle are married.

1992

Barack begins teaching at the University of Chicago Law School.

August 2008

Barack is nominated as the Democratic candidate for the presidency.

February 10, 2007

Barack announces his candidacy for the office of president of the United States of America.

2006

Barack's second book, *The Audacity of Hope*, is published.

November 2004

Barack is elected to the U.S. Senate.

President-elect Barack Obama hugs his daughter Malia at his election night celebration in Grant Park, Chicago, on November 4, 2008. Watching his acceptance speech, Malia realized that her dad was actually going to be president and the whole family would soon move to the White House.

1

My Daddy, the President

On the most important day of her life, 10-year-old Malia Obama was responsible for getting herself out of bed and selecting the clothes she would wear—as always. She set her alarm clock even earlier than usual because she and her little sister Natasha would be leaving to watch their parents vote in the presidential election at 7:30 in the morning on November 4, 2008.

Malia, who is tall for her age and cool by nature, is three years older than her sister, whose nickname is Sasha. Both girls were ready to leave their large, three-story brick home in the Hyde Park section of Chicago to go to nearby Shoesmith Elementary School where their parents, Barack and Michelle Obama, would cast their votes in a race that featured their father—a candidate for president of the United States.

When the family arrived at the polling place they were greeted by a long line of voters eager for their own chance to cast their ballots. Many of them planned to vote for Malia's father as the first African-American candidate to run for president. Also waiting for the family were newspaper and television reporters whose job was to capture the historic moment on film and in stories that would run in the next day's newspapers.

A SWEET MOMENT

Upon their arrival, Malia and her family were sent to the head of the line where, as she looked on, her parents, standing in adjacent voting booths, voted for Barack Obama for president and Joseph Biden Jr. for vice president. To be sure, it was a sweet moment made even more so by having Malia by her father's side. Barack said,

❝ The journey ends, but voting with my daughters, that was a big deal. ❞

After greeting some of their neighbors who had come out to vote, Malia's mother dropped her off at the private elementary

Family Rules

Malia's parents are big believers in rules that she is expected to follow to the letter. In addition to setting her own alarm clock every day to get up for school and putting out the clothes she intends to wear the next morning, Malia is also expected to make her own bed, clean up her toys, set the table, and clear away the dishes. Her parents expect her to avoid arguing with her sister and whining, be in bed at 8:30 P.M. most nights, and make do with an allowance of $1 a week.

And although Malia now lives in the "coolest house in America," the rules her parents have made her live by have not changed that much.

Malia and her younger sister, Sasha, look on as their mom and dad, Barack and Michelle Obama, vote at Shoesmith Elementary School in Chicago on election day, November 4, 2008. Barack later said that having his daughters there when he voted was very important to him.

school she attended, University of Chicago Lab School. Even though this was the day her father had the opportunity to become the 44th president of the United States, Malia was not allowed to miss school.

While Malia was at school focusing on classroom work, her father and mother were involved in more hectic pursuits. With the clock ticking down, Barack did some last-minute campaigning in Indiana and interviews with reporters. Then he did something really unusual that no other presidential candidate has ever done on election day—he played hoops with a group of friends so he could chill. Soccer may be Malia's favorite sport, but her dad is jazzed by basketball, a sport he played at Punahou High School in

Hawaii when he was known on the court as "Barry O'Bomber." For the Democratic senator from Illinois, playing basketball on election day was a tradition he had established when he first ran for public office.

After saying goodbye to Malia, her mother went home. In the comfort of the family's Georgian revival style mansion Michelle Obama spent several hours being interviewed by television stations across the country, doing all she could to help her husband seal the deal with voters on the last day that mattered.

When school was over, Malia had her hair done so she would look her best for the celebration that was sure to take place that night whether her dad won or lost. Later she would wear a red silk dress with a bow around the waist and black tights, which would match both her mother's red and black dress and her sister's all black ensemble.

The family ate a quiet dinner together and waited until 10 P.M. to go to the Chicago hotel suite in which friends and family members were watching the voting returns. The mood was high because a strong turnout had propelled two-thirds of eligible voters to the polls and the Obama-Biden ticket was capturing states that had previously gone Republican. It was apparent that Republican presidential candidate John McCain and vice presidential candidate Sarah Palin had been defeated.

GRANT PARK

As the time approached for Barack to give his victory speech the family headed over to Grant Park, where 240,000 Obama supporters had gathered, some coming from far away and arriving at the park as early as the day before to get a good spot to view history in the making. Ervin Ricks, a Chicago resident in his fifties who was there, commented on the significance of the event,

> **" I figured progress would come about with a senator here or a governor there, but I didn't think the top rung was for anybody but a Caucasian. "**

There was an exuberant, joyful vibe to the multiracial crowd that stood shoulder to shoulder swaying to music as they waited patiently for the Obama family to come out. And tears were streaming down the faces of some people who believed that the day's events were nothing short of a miracle come true.

Shielded from the crowds, Malia and her family were gathered together under a plastic tent waiting for their turn to go on stage. Then the moment came. An announcer said,

An emotional crowd of more than 240,000 people celebrates history in the making as President-elect Barack Obama gives his acceptance speech in Grant Park, Chicago. Some people at the event had never believed an African American could be elected president.

Barack, Sasha, Malia, and Michelle Obama greet the crowd at the election night rally in Grant Park, Chicago. Malia waved to the crowd and seemed comfortable in the spotlight as the Obamas were introduced as the next first family of America.

"Ladies and gentlemen, the next first family of the United States of America!"

Malia held hands with her mother and sister as the family walked out on the stage to the roar of the crowd who had waited for hours to see them. Malia smiled and waved to the mass of people before her, perfectly at ease at being in the spotlight.

Then taking a seat with her mother and sister, Malia listened in surprise and delight as she got a shout-out from the man on the stage whom America had fallen in love with. Said Barack,

> **❝ Sasha and Malia, I love you so much. You have earned the new puppy that will be coming to the White House with us. ❞**

First Puppy

Malia and her sister got a campaign promise from their father even before he announced he was running for president. The girls asked for—and were told they could have—a puppy whether their father won the election or lost.

There was one slight catch, however. Because Malia has asthma and is allergic to dog fur their puppy had to come from a breed that does not make Malia sneeze, have teary eyes, or find it hard to breathe.

When word about Malia's asthma broke, the news media were filled with ordinary Americans making suggestions about what type of puppy should go to the White House with the family. One puppy offered to the family was a Peruvian hairless dog that is completely bald, and some might say funny looking. For her part, Malia helped in the search, researching dog breeds on the Internet to find a puppy that would not aggravate her asthma.

Malia Obama plays with a puppy. During her father's acceptance speech, Malia was thrilled to hear Barack say the family would be getting a new puppy when they moved to the White House. She immediately started researching dog breeds that would not aggravate her asthma.

Marian Robinson, Michelle's mother and Malia's grandmother. Before moving to Washington to be near her granddaughters, Robinson joked, "The White House reminds me of a museum. How do you sleep in a museum?" However, she added, "They will need me, so I'm going to be there."

② A Story of Two Grandmothers

Malia's **maternal** grandmother, Marian Robinson, would do absolutely anything for her granddaughters—even move to Washington, D.C., to be near them despite loving her own home in Chicago. That modest home, where Michelle Obama grew up, is located just ten minutes away from the Hyde Park mansion where the Obama family lives.

When Malia's parents could not be with her because of campaign demands, Robinson stepped in, sometimes bringing Malia and Sasha to stay at her house and gladly chauffeuring

Malia to soccer games, dance and drama lessons, play dates, and school.

Were it not for the presence of Robinson, who is in her seventies, it is unlikely that Barack would have considered running for president. Michelle's brother, Craig, a college basketball coach, said,

> **❝The sole reason Michelle was willing to campaign at all was because she knows that Mom is there to help take care of the girls.❞**

DOING WHAT GRANDMOTHERS DO

Spending time with Robinson is a treat for Malia because her grandmother lets the family rules slide for the sake of having fun. Robinson said,

> **❝I have candy, they stay up late—come to my house, they watch TV as long as they want to. We'll play games until the wee hours. I do everything that grandmothers do that they're not supposed to.❞**

Of course Robinson was not so laid back with Michelle, who was born in 1964, or her older brother when they were growing up on the South Side of Chicago in a small apartment. Robinson told Michelle and Craig to keep it real—work hard and hit the books hard. As for Marian Robinson, she worked mostly secretarial jobs while her husband, Fraser, a descendant of slaves from South Carolina, worked at a water treatment plant. Marian and Fraser did not go to college but made sure that their children did. Michelle is a graduate of Princeton University in New Jersey and Harvard University in Massachusetts, where she received a law degree.

Fraser, who suffered from **multiple sclerosis** and died in 1991, never got the chance to see his pretty granddaughters or discover the personality traits they share with his wife. Michelle said,

The Robinsons pose for a family portrait. Fraser holds Craig while mother Marian holds baby Michelle. Marian and Fraser Robinson expected their children to work and study hard, but according to Craig, Marian also loved to laugh. Growing up, he said, "There was always humor."

"My mother's love has always been the sustaining force for our family. One of my greatest joys is seeing her integrity, her compassion, and her intelligence reflected in my daughters."

When Barack met Michelle, one of the things he appreciated most about her was her solid family life. When they married in 1992 they decided to model their future family on the Robinsons rather than the rootless life of the Obamas. Barack, whose parents were divorced when he was a young boy, was raised by his mother, Stanley Ann, but also lived with his grandparents in Hawaii for many years.

Baby Stanley Ann Dunham, Barack's mother and Malia's grand-mother, poses with her parents, Madelyn and Stanley Dunham, for a family portrait in Kansas in the mid-1940s. Although the Dunhams were unhappy at first that Stanley Ann married an African man, they later helped raise Barack and always made him feel loved and supported.

A WHITE WOMAN FROM KANSAS

Like Malia, Barack also had a close relationship with his grand-mother, Madelyn Dunham, a white woman from Kansas, whom he called "Toot." Toot is an abbreviation for the way the word for grandmother is pronounced in Hawaiian. Later, when Stanley Ann died of cancer, Toot and Barack's grandfather, Stanley, became more like parents to him.

Toot was initially unhappy when her daughter informed her that she was pregnant and going to marry a **charismatic** black man from Kenya. That young man's name was Barack Obama Sr. Stanley Ann and Barack Sr. met when they were both students at the University of Hawaii; they began dating, and soon fell in love. Their son, Barack Hussein Obama Jr., was born in 1961 in Hawaii.

After just a few years of marriage, Barack Obama Sr. left Hawaii to study at Harvard. Eventually he returned to Kenya, having little to do with his wife or child. He never got to know Barack, but his

How Kenyans Celebrated the Election

Although he was born in the United States, Barack Obama is considered a native son of a small village where his step-grandmother "Mama" Sarah Obama lives; his father, Barack Obama Sr., is buried, and several of his half-brothers and other family members make their homes. As a result, America's presidential election, which otherwise would have passed by unnoticed there, was the talk of the town as Mama Sarah's fellow villagers held tightly to the promise that one of their own could be elected president of the United States.

In the village where televisions are not common, hundreds of people sat up all night watching a screen put up for the occasion by the local television company. The moment Barack earned enough electoral votes to capture the presidency a woman yelled, "Barry has won! Barry has won!" using the name Barack used to go by when he was a boy. Then came singing, dancing, and feasting. Mwai Kibaki, president of Kenya, placed a call to Barack in the U.S., offering him his country's congratulations and alerting him to the fact that the next day would be a national holiday—in Kenya.

absence in the boy's life had a profound effect. Barack decided that he would be an involved father when he had children.

Stanley Ann remarried, this time to a man from Indonesia with whom she had a daughter, Maya. The family spent several years living in Indonesia, but by the time Barack reached fifth grade, his mother sent him and his half-sister back to Hawaii to live with her parents. Stanley Ann eventually divorced her second husband and returned to Hawaii for a brief time. When she once again said she was moving back to Indonesia Barack decided to remain in Hawaii to live with his grandparents and finish high school.

Barack poses with his father in 1971, when Barack Sr. made his only return visit to the U.S. Barack never saw his father again. Because his parents were divorced and his father was not involved in his upbringing, Barack has always wanted to be a hands-on father to his daughters.

Toot was a remarkable woman who had been an aircraft inspector during World War II and later went on to become one of the first female bank vice presidents in America.

In his autobiography, *Dreams from My Father*, Barack wrote about his grandparents,

> **❝They had poured all their lingering hopes into my success. Never had they given me any reason to doubt their love; I doubted if they ever would.❞**

Although Malia never got to know her great-grandfather Stanley, she did come to know Toot well because her family frequently vacationed in Hawaii so they could see her. Two weeks before the presidential election when Barack learned that Toot was dying of cancer, he cleared his campaign schedule to spend an entire day saying goodbye to the woman who had been like a second mother to him. Just two days before the election she died at age 86.

The Mansion Books Built

How many children can say that their father is both a best-selling author and winner of a Grammy Award? Malia's father's books, *The Audacity of Hope*, which came out in 2006, and *Dreams from My Father*, which was originally published in 1995 and reprinted in 2005, have been flying off book shelves since the 2008 election. Shortly after the election, *The Audacity of Hope* was the second most purchased book on the online bookseller Amazon.com and the third most popular book on the *New York Times* list of bestsellers. One online auction site sold a 1995 autographed copy of *Dreams from My Father* for more than $5,000. The audio book editions of both Barack's books won Grammy Awards for Best Spoken Word Album.

Even before the election, before he was well known, Barack's books provided significant income for the Obama family and helped the family afford their Hyde Park home, which the Obamas purchased in 2005 for $1.6 million.

Baby Malia poses with mom Michelle Obama. When Malia was born, new dad Barack described her as having "big hypnotic eyes." He felt his new responsibilities as a dad so strongly that he drove Michelle and baby Malia home from the hospital very, very slowly.

3

Big Hypnotic Eyes

B arack and Michelle welcomed their new baby daughter, Malia Ann Obama, to the world on July 4, 1998. In his book, *The Audacity of Hope*, Barack described his first impressions of his new daughter:

❝ Malia was born, a Fourth of July baby, so calm and so beautiful, with big hypnotic eyes that seemed to read the world the moment they opened. ❞

The birth of Malia dramatically changed the lives of her parents beginning with the ride home from the hospital, when Michelle recalls that Barack drove so slowly and carefully that she thought the family would never get home. In her speech before the 2008 Democratic National Convention she remembered,

"Barack is the same man who drove me and our new baby daughter [Malia] home from the hospital 10 years ago this summer, inching along at a snail's pace, peering cautiously at us in the rearview mirror, feeling the whole weight of our future in his hands."

Born on the Fourth of July

Malia Obama's birthday is July 4, which is Independence Day—the day in 1776 that America declared its independence from Great Britain. Independence Day is often called America's birthday.

Malia Obama isn't the only famous person born on Independence Day. Others who have celebrated their birthdays on July 4 include President Calvin Coolidge; George Steinbrenner, who owns the New York Yankees; playwright Neil Simon, who wrote *The Odd Couple* and other Broadway hits, and Louis B. Mayer, a pioneer in early moviemaking. Among the notable Americans who died on July 4 are three former presidents—John Adams, Thomas Jefferson and James Monroe.

Barack had been elected to the Illinois State Senate two years before Malia was born, and he spent a lot of time in the state capital of Springfield. The new addition to the family plus the demands of Barack's career created a lot of tension between Malia's parents. Michelle told Barack in no uncertain terms that he needed to make his family a priority. He was stung when she accused him of thinking only of himself and forcing her to raise a family on her own.

However, Barack came to realize that Michelle was right to complain about his absences and that she was carrying more than her share of responsibility for their little girl. He remembered,

> **❝** If Malia got sick or the babysitter failed to show up, it was she who, more often than not, had to get on the phone to cancel a meeting at work. **❞**

PUTTING FAMILY FIRST

With both her parents working, Malia was sometimes looked after by nannies. This seemed normal to the young girl as did the fact that her father was away more than he was home.

Although Malia was too young to know anything about the incident, when she was 18 months old her father put her welfare first when he missed an important vote in the state senate.

Barack Obama, with help from his daughter Malia, casts his vote in 2000. When tension arose between Barack and Michelle because of his frequent absences on political business, Barack realized he needed to change his priorities and spend more time with his family.

Malia peeks out from behind the lectern as Barack delivers his concession speech after losing a congressional election in 2000. Barack's decision to stay with Malia when she was sick, instead of voting on a gun control bill, played a part in his loss in that election.

Although he supported the gun control measure that was up for a vote, the Safe Neighborhoods bill, he refused to cut short the family vacation in Hawaii to fly back to Springfield to cast his vote. Malia was sick and Barack had not been home much in the months leading up to the trip. He knew Michelle would be angry if he abandoned the long-planned vacation for work.

Unfortunately, there was major political fallout over his decision. The Safe Neighborhoods bill was narrowly defeated and Barack was roundly criticized for his absence. He told reporters,

> **❝I cannot sacrifice the health or well-being of my daughter for politics. I had to make a decision based on what I felt was appropriate for my daughter and my wife.❞**

Meanwhile, the timing of the controversy hurt him as well. Barack was then running for a seat in the U.S. House against popular incumbent Bobby Rush, whose son had just been murdered in an act of gun violence. Voters felt sorry for Congressman Rush while coming to the conclusion that Barack didn't think gun violence was that big a deal. Barack's failure to help the Safe Neighborhoods bill pass played a role in his loss in the election against Rush.

On June 10, 2001, Malia's sister Sasha joined the family. Barack remained in the Illinois legislature where he was re-elected in 2002. During his second term he was selected chairman of the Senate Health and Human Services Committee, and with the backing of a new Democratic majority in the state senate, Barack was able to assist in the passage of new legislation that helped people without medical insurance, protected the rights of people who were arrested, and limited the power of **lobbyists** to influence politicians through campaign donations.

Still, Barack planned to run for higher office. In 2004, he ran for the U.S. Senate. After beating two other candidates in the Democratic **primary**, he prepared for the fall election against a Republican opponent. That summer, Democratic presidential nominee John Kerry asked Barack if he would give the **keynote**

speech at the party's national convention—one that would come before Kerry was formally nominated by the assembled **delegates**. Obama had come to Kerry's notice after the younger man campaigned for him and demonstrated that he could command attention when he spoke.

PRESIDENTIAL RUMBLINGS

As Obama took the stage at the Fleet Center in Boston to give that keynote address he was a virtual unknown. Yet when he left the stage just 17 minutes later, after sharing the remarkable story of

Barack holds Malia and Michelle carries Sasha in celebration after Barack won election to the U.S. Senate in 2004. He became the fifth African-American Senator in U.S. history. That same year, Barack gave the keynote speech at the Democratic National Convention, which propelled him onto the national political stage.

his life with his fellow Democrats, people were already talking about whether he would one day run for the presidency himself.

That night Malia's father began his speech by saying,

❝I stand here today, grateful for the diversity of my heritage, aware that my parents' dreams live on in my two precious daughters. I stand here knowing that my story is part of the larger American story, that I owe a debt to all of those who came before me, and that, in no other country on earth, is my story even possible.❞

That fall, Barack won the Senate seat. And a few months later, Malia and her sister stood right beside their father when he was sworn into office as a senator from Illinois by Vice President Dick Cheney. That year they also visited the White House for the first time. Rather than being impressed by their good luck at setting foot where few children have gone before them, Malia and Sasha couldn't wait to leave. They were bored that time except for the brief moments they spent playing with President George W. Bush's dog Barney. But the second time they visited the White House, as guests of President Bush's twin daughters Barbara and Jenna, they had a ball jumping on the beds when no adults were looking.

The Obamas share a relaxing moment. Even during the presidential campaign, the family had time to talk together. Michelle has said, "Our girls love to talk. . . . They feel confident in their own opinions because we value them [even] if they're silly or wrong or a little off."

Standing in Lincoln's Shadow

Before Barack Obama declared himself a candidate for the presidency in 2007, he talked to his wife and daughters to make sure the entire family was willing to go along with the sacrifices that would have to be made. It would mean even less time for the family to be together than before.

Eventually everyone came on board, although Malia had a question for him. "Shouldn't you be vice president first?" she asked. Barack agreed that being vice president was one path to the presidency but not the only one.

Michelle recalled what went through her mind when Barack first raised the possibility of running for president. She said,

" I took myself down every dark road you could go on, just to prepare myself before we jumped out there. Are we emotionally, financially ready for this? I dreamed out all of the scenarios. The bottom line is, man, the little sacrifice we have to make is nothing compared to the possibility of what we could do if this catches on. **"**

Presidential Candidates' Children

Malia and her sister Sasha were not the only young children with a father running for president in 2007. Nine-year-old Emma Claire Edwards and seven-year-old Jack Edwards, children of Barack's opponent Democrat John Edwards, were often at their parents' side during primary season. Christopher Dodd, Sam Brownback, and Fred D. Thompson, who were also presidential primary candidates, each had very young children. All of these children had one thing in common: the need to cope with absent fathers.

During the summer of 2007 when they were off from school, Malia and Sasha sometimes traveled with their parents in a rented RV so the family could be together while Barack campaigned. They made seven campaign stops with Mom and Dad, unsuccessfully looking for moose in New Hampshire, and trying out the rides at the Iowa State Fair. Whenever possible, Michelle and Barack arranged fun things for the girls like trips to zoos and museums, as well as spur-of-the-moment stops for ice cream.

When it came time to make his decision public, Barack chose an inspiring backdrop. On a cold February day he stood outside of the Old State Capitol Building in Springfield, Illinois, on the exact spot where Abraham Lincoln had also launched his presidential campaign. Barack told the world why he was running for president of the United States even though he had less experience in government than the two other politicians who had already announced their candidacies: Senator Hillary Clinton of New York and former Senator John Edwards of North Carolina. He said,

Sasha, Barack, Malia, and Michelle wave to the crowd after Barack announced his candidacy for president at the Old State Capitol in Springfield, Illinois, February 10, 2007, two days before Abraham Lincoln's birthday. After Barack's presidential campaign began, the family would have fewer private moments together.

❝I recognize there is a certain presumptuousness in this—a certain audacity—to this announcement. I know that I haven't spent a lot of time learning the ways of Washington. But I've been there long enough to know that the ways of Washington must change.❞

The Obama-Lincoln Connection

Barack Obama is a great admirer of Abraham Lincoln. Both are from Illinois and both are lawyers who arrived in Washington with little political experience. In addition to announcing his candidacy where Lincoln started his political career, Barack has frequently mentioned Lincoln in speeches he has given, inviting comparisons between the two men.

One of the things Obama admired about Lincoln, who came to the presidency when the country was on the brink of a civil war, was the 16th president's willingness to bring some of his opponents into his cabinet. Barack has taken a page out of the Lincoln playbook by appointing his former opponent, Hillary Clinton, secretary of state.

Lincoln was also known as a great orator, uniting the country by delivering the Gettysburg Address, helping heal the divisiveness of war. Barack is also a skillful speechwriter and speaker. Matthew Teague, writing in *Philadelphia* magazine, described Obama's speeches this way:

"To a population used to eighth-grade **rhetoric**, the gorgeous loops and rhythms of Obama's **oratory** are intellectually dazzling. And yet his popular, ever-simple phrases—'Yes we can'—reduce the message to something a toddler could grasp."

MICHELLE AND ANGELINA

Shortly after the announcement, Malia's dad went on the road, crisscrossing the country as he started to put his campaign together. For the rest of 2007 and for much of the 2008 primary election season her father would be away from home. Both her mother and father would increasingly be receiving favorable and unfavorable media attention. Seeing her father's face on a magazine cover didn't seem to affect Malia too much. It was simply the way things were. In fact she probably got a bigger kick out of seeing her mother's photograph in *People* magazine in close proximity to actress Angelina Jolie than in seeing her father's image on the cover of *Time*.

PARIS MATCH

"PLUS BELLE
LA VIE"
LE FEUILLETON
PHENOMENE QUI
FAIT PEUR AUX JT

**CARLA REÇOIT
CHARLES ET CAMILLA
A L'ELYSEE**

OTAGES FRANÇAIS
CELLULE DE CRISE
AU QUAI D'ORSAY

MICHELLE ET BARACK OBAMA
**UN COUPLE GLAMOUR
A LA TETE DE L'AMERIQUE**
AVEC LEURS PETITES FILLES,

Michelle and Barack Obama grace the cover of *Paris Match*
magazine. As her father's campaign progressed, Malia's parents
appeared on more and more magazine covers, but all the publicity
didn't bother Malia very much. She thought it was simply part
of the campaign process.

Limited to just one hour of television time a day, Malia did not have a lot of exposure to broadcast news about her mom and dad—except when she stayed at her grandmother's house. On one such occasion Malia heard something about Michelle that confused her. While making a speech in Wisconsin in early 2008, Michelle said, "For the first time in my adult lifetime, I am really proud of my country, and not just because Barack has done well, but because I think people are hungry for change."

Conservative **pundits** and other critics quickly jumped on those remarks, calling Michelle unpatriotic. And Cindy McCain, the wife of Republican presidential candidate John McCain, said, "I don't know about you, if you heard those words earlier, I'm very proud of my country."

Responding to the controversy over Michelle's words, Barack assured Malia that her mom loved America as much as anyone. Said Barack,

❝ When some folks were attacking Michelle, Malia just asked, 'What was that all about?' And we talked it through. She's completely confident about her mommy's wonderfulness. ❞

HAPPY TOGETHER

When daddy did manage to take a break from the politics, Malia and her sister did not want to talk about the campaign. As Michelle remembered,

❝ [When daddy comes home] they're like, 'Let me show you my soccer trophy. I don't really care what you do.' ❞

Malia and Barack used their rare time together to read the books about boy wizard Harry Potter as well as the books in the *Twilight* series in which a teenage girl falls in love with a handsome young vampire. They also spent time outdoors talking to each other. Whether Barack was in town or not, Malia's days went flying by with school, piano lessons, soccer, and acting classes occupying her thoughts. She relaxed by listening—and dancing to—Beyonce, the Jonas Brothers, Hannah Montana, and dreaming about her own future as an actress.

Despite Malia's lack of interest in what her father did for a living, Barack's message of change was starting to resonate with voters who were weary of the war in Iraq, which he had opposed since Congress authorized an invasion of the Middle

Malia and Barack on a carnival ride at the Iowa State Fair, August 16, 2007. Even on the campaign trail, Barack took time to do fun things with his daughters. As Michelle said, "He's an incredible husband and father. Not sure if the world knows yet, but they should."

East country in 2003. Overall, Barack had also been criticizing the direction the United States had taken during the eight years of President Bush's administration.

By the end of 2007, Barack had raised more money than any of the other Democratic candidates; while the other candidates each had $75 million in their coffers, Barack had nearly $105 million, which gave him the luxury of hiring more staff members and spending more money on advertising than his competitors. The amount of money a candidate is able to raise reflects the enthusiasm ordinary people have for that candidate, particularly if the donations come in small amounts, as Barack's did. Flush

Malia, Barack, Sasha, and Michelle, at a campaign stop in Iowa, January 1, 2008. Appearances such as this helped voters see Barack's solid connection to his family. In addition to liking his message of change, many people supported him because they felt he was a good family man.

with cash to spend, Barack's campaign was in a good position to take on his more experienced rivals.

In early January 2008, Barack scored his first important victory when he won the Iowa **caucuses**, which was the first occasion in the presidential contest in which the candidates faced the voters. A few days later, Senator Clinton recovered to win the New Hampshire primary, but Barack soon emerged as the front-runner. In February, he ran off an impressive string of 12 straight primary and caucus victories, giving him a lead over Clinton that he would never relinquish. By early June, he wrapped up the nomination, which was officially awarded to him in late August at the Democratic National Convention.

Hillary Rodham Clinton

When the primary season began, U.S. Senator Hillary Rodham Clinton of New York appeared to have all the advantages. A former first lady, Hillary is married to former president Bill Clinton. After leaving the White House in 2001, she served in the U.S. Senate. She is the only former first lady to win election to Congress.

Hillary Clinton was regarded as the first female candidate for the presidency with a good chance at winning and had a dedicated following of women who hoped that she would break the glass ceiling that has kept a woman from occupying America's highest office. (In politics and business the glass ceiling is said to separate women from the most important jobs: they can look up and see the big jobs ahead of them, but they can't break through the glass ceiling that separates them from those positions.) In addition, many influential Democratic Party leaders had agreed to back her candidacy from the start.

Clinton focused her campaign on her Washington experience. At age 61, she is 13 years older than Barack. She hammered him for his relative lack of experience and hinted that his soaring rhetoric was nothing more than a cover-up for vague ideas about how he would change America. After losing the nomination, she campaigned for Barack, and after the election accepted a cabinet position as secretary of state.

Michelle, Malia, Sasha, and Barack at a campaign rally in Des Moines, Iowa, May 20, 2008. Even though bigger and bigger crowds came to see her father, Malia realized she was not the focus of their attention. She just waved and then let Barack take center stage.

SHE'S OUT OF THERE

As the campaign continued Malia saw how her father was able to draw big crowds to his campaign appearances. But being a part of all that hoopla did not go to her head. She said,

> **" Those people aren't there to see me. They just think I'm cute. So I just wave and smile, and then I'm out of there. "**

Michelle continued to do all she could to make Malia's life as normal as possible. Her rule was not to be away from her daughters for more than a day at a time, and sometimes that meant hopping on a plane after a busy day of making appearances on her husband's behalf, tired but determined to tuck Malia and her sister into bed. She would continue to do so as the Obamas moved into the general election in the fall of 2008.

The Illinois Connection

Abraham Lincoln and Barack Obama are not the only presidents who could point to an Illinois connection. Ronald Reagan was born in 1911 in Tampico, Illinois, a small town about 100 miles west of Chicago. The Reagans lived in a small apartment over a bakery. The Reagan family moved around quite a bit, but stayed in the state until Reagan was a young adult. He attended Eureka College near Bloomington. Before he became a politician Reagan had a successful career as a Hollywood actor appearing in such films as *Bedtime for Bonzo* and *Knute Rockne All American*. Reagan parlayed his fame as an actor into two successful terms as governor of California before running for the presidency in 1980.

President Ulysses S. Grant lived in Illinois before he commanded the Union troops during the Civil War. Grant had moved to the town of Galena to work in his family's business. After the war his fellow townspeople threw him a party with fireworks and a parade. They also bought him a new house, where he lived until he was elected president in 1869.

Sasha, Michelle, and Malia at the 2008 Democratic National Convention in Denver, Colorado, August 25, 2008. Michelle hoped that Malia would think it was a cool surprise to speak to Barack via satellite, but Malia had hoped the surprise would be to see the Jonas Brothers.

5

Heading to the White House

E very four years, officials of the Democratic Party gather at a national convention to formally nominate their candidate for president and vice president and pump up supporters around the country. On August 25, 2008, the first day of the convention, Malia was with her mother in Denver. That night Michelle addressed the entire assembly.

When Michelle finished her speech, which was well received by the crowd, she told Malia she had a surprise for her. Malia's ears perked up as she considered the possibilities. She had wanted to stay at home in Chicago because her favorite musical act was due in town, and suddenly her hopes rose. "Is it the Jonas Brothers?" she asked. It wasn't enough that she had plastered pictures of

Nick, Kevin, and Joe on her bedroom wall at home and that their music dominated her iPod. She wanted to see them in person.

Michelle was speechless. The surprise she had in mind was a special appearance by Malia's father whose image was going to be beamed to the convention by satellite. Michelle thought her daughter would find this bit of technical wizardry cool, but Barack was no Jonas brother even if he did understand the power of using the latest gadgetry to get his message across.

The Jonas Brothers—(from left) Nick, Joe, and Kevin—perform in Irvine, California, in May 2008. They are Malia's favorite band; her bedroom features their posters and her iPod is full of their music. She hopes to invite them to the White House some day.

Celebrities Love White House Kids

One of the totally awesome things about living in the White House is that the first family can invite any celebrity they want to visit or entertain them, and there is a good chance that their invitation will be accepted.

Malia met the Jonas Brothers and played ping-pong with the singers when her mom was on Ellen DeGeneres's television show. The brothers have already indicated that they plan to accept the Obamas' invitation and visit the White House. Joe Jonas is on record saying that Malia and Sasha are sweet. Malia and Sasha have also been invited to appear on their favorite television show, *Hannah Montana*, and if their parents don't think that is a good idea, the girls can just visit the set and meet the show's cast members.

Indeed, the Obama campaign was the first to use technology in a big way. In addition to maintaining a way-cool Web site, Barack had his campaign workers use computers to keep track of volunteers and newly registered voters. He became a regular fixture on YouTube and used a webcam to check in with Malia and Sasha during his nightly phone calls to them.

Back at the convention before the delegates officially gave Barack the nomination, there were other speeches. Hillary Clinton, once Barack's formidable rival, gave a rousing talk to sway her ardent supporters to put away their bitter feelings and focus on Barack's candidacy. Senator Clinton's husband, former president Bill Clinton, spoke too as did Senator Ted Kennedy, brother of the late president John F. Kennedy and an elder statesman in his own right, who came to the event even though he had recently been diagnosed with brain cancer.

DELEGATE SERVICE DAY

On the third day of the convention, Malia joined Sasha and their mother in assembling care packages for troops serving in Iraq and Afghanistan. Michelle was the co-chair of the Democratic National Convention's Delegate Service Day. That was the day that delegates were asked to participate in service-oriented projects that included canned food sorting, painting at local schools, serving meals at shelters, reading to children, tree planting, and park maintenance. The projects were organized at various sites throughout the Denver area, allowing delegates to both contribute to and celebrate the people and organizations making positive change in the city that hosted the Democratic National Convention.

After having experienced the positive results of the Delegate Service Day projects, delegates were encouraged to get involved or recommit to service upon returning to their home communities, helping to inspire millions more Americans to lives of service.

QUOTING MARTIN LUTHER KING JR.

On the final night of the convention Barack accepted his party's nomination at an outdoor rally in a football stadium packed with 84,000 people. Referencing a famous speech given 45 years before by the civil rights leader, the late Reverend Martin Luther King Jr., Barack said:

> **❝America, we cannot turn back. Not with so much work to be done. Not with so many children to educate, and so many veterans to care for. Not with an economy to fix and cities to rebuild and farms to save. Not with so many families to protect and so many lives to mend. America, we cannot turn back.**
>
> **We cannot walk alone. At this moment, in this election, we must pledge once more to march into the future. Let us keep that promise—that American promise—and in the words of Scripture hold firmly, without wavering, to the hope that we confess. Thank you, God bless you, and God bless the United States of America.❞**

In the coming weeks voters would get the chance to learn more about Barack and his Republican opponent, John McCain, as well as their positions on important issues, during three televised

Michelle, Malia, and Sasha assemble care packages for troops at the Democratic National Convention's Delegate Service Day, August 27, 2008. Malia enjoyed helping in her father's campaign and participating in good causes such as supporting the troops.

Barack Obama gives his acceptance speech at the Democratic National Convention held at Mile High Stadium in Denver, August 28, 2008. A crowd of 84,000 people heard him refer to the ideals of Rev. Martin Luther King, Jr., when Barack encouraged the nation to march together into the future.

presidential debates. In all of them Barack appeared cool, calm, and collected, while McCain seemed at times wooden, restless, frustrated, and upset.

FIST BUMP FLAP

It was clear that Barack and McCain were of different generations, and even some of the little gestures between Barack and Michelle were subject to misrepresentation. Malia's parents were captured on camera giving each other a "fist bump." What might have been viewed as a hip thing to do suddenly became suspicious, as one Fox News anchor expressed the opinion that the Obamas had snuck in a "terrorist fist jab" right under America's nose. Michelle subsequently went on the popular daytime talk show *The View* to explain that touching fists was no more radical than giving someone a high five and she proceeded to bump fists with *The View's* co-hosts.

The fist bump incident no doubt had a familiar ring to Malia, who previously had given her dad much needed instructions on how to greet her friends without causing her embarrassment. Malia did so after she introduced her dad to her new BFFs and he reached out to shake their hands. She admonished her father,

> **"You really don't shake kids' hands that much. . . . You just wave or say hi."**

Besides giving her dad instructions on how to be cool, Malia at least occasionally worried that her father's presidential campaign would interfere with her life in other ways.

With a hefty advertising budget, Malia's father and his running mate, Senator Joe Biden, were constantly appearing in television commercials explaining why they were better suited to run the country than McCain and Palin. One night in October, as the election grew near, Barack bought time on all the major television networks to air an **infomercial**. At the Obama kitchen table, as he was explaining the purpose of going on TV, Malia wandered by. Michelle explains,

> **"She says, 'You're gonna be on all the TV? Are you gonna interrupt my TV?' And Barack says, 'No, we didn't buy time on Disney and Nick.' And she says 'Oh good.' And she got up and walked away."**

Of course November 4, 2008, election day, was the last day the political advertisements were aired. By the time the media blitz was over that night Barack had captured 53 percent of the vote and became the first African American to be elected president of the United States.

SCHOOL CONTINUES TO RULE

Although she stayed up late on election night, Malia still went to school the next day and her parents took time out to attend the parent-teacher conference at Malia's soon-to-be former school.

Malia and her family would be moving to the White House a mere two months later and needed to select a new school fast. Michelle, Malia, and Sasha visited several private schools in the Washington area, selecting Sidwell Friends, the same prep school attended by Chelsea Clinton, daughter of Bill and Hillary Clinton.

During the same trip they were invited to the White House by the Bush family to tour their future living quarters. This time Malia wasn't bored because Jenna and Barbara Bush, the president's twin daughters, gave her an insider's tour of the White House.

Barbara and Jenna's mother, Laura, remembered that day well. She said,

❝It was fun for the girls to get to show them not only [their rooms], but the way the big cross hall can be an obstacle course for little kids to run up and down, and the solarium ramp that you can slide down on your bottom. So they showed them all the special tricks.❞

A Kid's Paradise

The White House is like no other home in America. It has 31 bathrooms, a pool, a bowling alley, a movie theater with popcorn maker, tennis courts (which Malia will use), and it will also soon have a basketball court for her dad, the president, who played hoops in high school.

There are secret staircases and lots of places to explore, chefs who make favorite desserts when the members of the first family have a bad day, and plenty of room for playing Uno and charades, two favorite Obama family pastimes.

Michelle, Sasha, Malia, and Barack wave at a campaign rally in Pueblo, Colorado, three days before the presidential election. Although the whole family stayed up late on election night, Malia had to go to school the next day, just as she had throughout most of the campaign.

Malia was able to select her new bedroom and decorate it the way she wanted. She also laid claim to the desk President Lincoln used to sign the Emancipation Proclamation—the document that freed the slaves—where she said she would forever more do her homework because "it would give me big ideas."

The family moved into the White House on January 20, 2008— the day of Barack's inauguration—at the conclusion of what turned out to be an all-day celebration. That morning, Malia and Sasha watched as their father put his hand on the same Bible Lincoln used and was sworn in as the 44th president of the United States. Malia and Sasha viewed the event while seated in a grandstand erected on the grounds of the U.S. Capitol along with

Issue 719
November 24, 2008

WEEKL

TWILIGHT!
Meet the
Hot Stars

Obama with
Malia (left)
and Sasha

BARACK OBAMA'S GIRLS

'I Think I'm a Pretty Cool Dad'

- Barack & Michelle's plan to keep their family life normal
- First Daughters' excitement & fears:

$3.99US $4.79CAN

47>

Malia, Barack, and Sasha on the cover of *Us* magazine. The girls are finding that the White House is a cool place to be together as a family. Michelle says, "Our girls are the center of Barack's and my world. They're the reason he ran for president."

some 1,600 other dignitaries including Supreme Court justices and former presidents. Meanwhile, hundreds of thousands of people crowded downtown Washington to watch the swearing-in ceremony as well as the inaugural parade.

The city was jammed with ordinary people who wanted to see the first African-American president take the oath of office. Others who could not get close enough to see the ceremony crowded around giant television screens installed nearby. After the ceremony and parade, the whole city celebrated with concerts and balls.

Radiance and Rosebud

The Secret Service—the federal agency that protects presidents and members of the first family—has code names for everyone in its charge. Malia's code name is Radiance and her little sister Sasha is Rosebud.

Soon after their father announced plans to run for president, Malia and Sasha began receiving protection from secret service agents who would accompany them when they went to school and, in Malia's case, to dance and acting classes. One mother, whose son became friends with Malia in drama class without realizing who she was, said the secret service agent who accompanied Malia looked like a regular dad. She was shocked when Malia showed up for the final performance with her real father.

Malia and Sasha became the youngest residents of the White House since the young children of President Kennedy occupied the executive mansion in the early 1960s. And, in doing so, Michelle got her wish when she said,

❝We want to make sure that we're upholding what the house stands for. But I couldn't help envisioning the girls running into their rooms and running down the hall with a dog. Our hope is that the White House will feel open and fun and full of life and energy.❞

1961   Father, Barack Obama, is born in Hawaii on August 4.

1964   Mother, Michelle Robinson, is born in Chicago on January 17.

1992   Parents marry.

1996   Barack wins a seat in the Illinois State Senate.

1998   Malia Obama is born in Chicago on July 4.

2001   Sister Natasha is born on June 10.

2004   Barack delivers keynote address at Democratic Convention.

Barack is elected to the U.S. Senate.

2007   Barack declares his candidacy for president of the United States.

2008   Barack is elected 44th president of the United States.

2009   The Obamas move into the White House.

- The Obamas brought their favorite pizza maker to Washington for the inaugural.

- Tropical Hawaii is the favorite Obama family vacation spot; Barack was born and grew up there. Malia visited her paternal grandmother there until her death just before the 2008 election.

- Malia loves ice cream, ping-pong, and soccer.

- Malia was often driven to school in Barack's Ford Escape hybrid; hybrid cars are considered to be "green vehicles" because they use a combination of gasoline and electric battery power.

- Malia is a good student who hopes someday to go to Yale University in Connecticut.

- Her godmother is civil rights leader Jesse Jackson's daughter, Sanita, who is a lifelong friend and former classmate of Michelle's.

- Malia's father used his cell phone to announce his choice for his vice presidential running mate, Joe Biden. Barack sent the message to 2.9 million people, which cost him $290,000.

- There are only about 20 Obama families in America, and most of them have roots in Kenya.

- Since the election a number of babies have been named for Barack, Michelle, Malia, and Sasha. That means the Obama family will be remembered for a long time to come.

caucuses—Some states hold elections by asking voters to gather together in groups and publicly demonstrate their choices for public offices by raising their hands or by being physically counted. This replaces the more familiar way of voting in the privacy of an election booth.

charismatic—Having a special magnetic charm or popular appeal, as seen in some politicians and celebrities.

delegates—Officials of the Republican and Democratic parties selected through primaries and caucuses and designated to cast votes to nominate presidential candidates at the party conventions, based on the number of popular votes the candidates received in the spring contests.

infomercial—Paid television commercial that usually lasts a half-hour or longer and may appear at first to be a regular television program. Airtime promotes the advertiser's selling points with no opposing viewpoints.

keynote speech—Most anticipated talk given at a convention or workshop, usually delivered at the beginning of the gathering by a highly respected individual. Its function is to set the tone for the meeting and serve as inspiration to the attendees.

lobbyists—People paid to bring the interests of their employers to the attention of politicians and other decision-makers.

maternal—Related through a mother; or quality or characteristic of a mother.

multiple sclerosis—Disease affecting 2.5 million people worldwide that causes changes to their nervous systems. Symptoms may include general tiredness and problems with balance, thinking, movement, and speech.

oratory—The art of speaking in public eloquently or effectively.

primary—Process used by many states to award delegates to presidential candidates; typically the voter casts a ballot in secret in a voting booth. Delegates are assigned to candidates based on the number of popular votes they receive.

pundits—Influential men or women who get paid for expressing their views in a clever way.

rhetoric—Words spoken or written eloquently or effectively, but often insincerely and only for the effect they will have.

White House—Official residence of the president and first family in Washington, D.C., portions of which are open to visits by the public. Considered the people's house, it is a symbol of American government.

Books and Periodicals

Connelly, Joel. "Search for the First Pooch Is No Joke," *Seattle-Post Intelligencer*, November 10, 2008.

McCormick, John. "Fun Things On Campaign Trail: Obama's Daughters Enjoy the Ride, But Not the Politicking," *Chicago Tribune*, May 29, 2007.

Obama, Barack. *Dreams from My Father: A Story of Race and Inheritance.* New York: Crown, 2004.

———. *The Audacity of Hope: Thoughts on Reclaiming the American Dream*. New York: Three Rivers Press, 2006.

Pallasch, Abdon M. "Obama Daughters' Opinions: White House Life Would Be Very Cool, Dad Talks Too Much," *Chicago Sun-Times*, July 9, 2008.

Strock, Ian Randal. *The President's Book of Lists: From Most to Least, Elected to Rejected, Worst to Cursed—Fascinating Facts About Our Chief Executive*. New York: Villard Books, 2008.

Wead, Doug. *All the President's Children: Triumph and Tragedy in the Lives of America's First Families*. New York: Atria Books, 2004.

Web Sites

www.huffingtonpost.com/2008/11/07/malia-obama-see-how-shes_ n_141836.html

Visitors can view photographs of Malia taken during the first eight years of her life, compiled by the Web site Huffington Post.

www.illinoishistory.gov/hs/old_capitol.htm

Illinois Historic Preservation Agency's Web site tells the story of the reconstructed Old State Capitol where Barack Obama announced his candidacy for president and Abraham Lincoln launched his campaign for the U.S. Senate in 1858. Students can follow links to see Lincoln's law office and other historic Illinois sites such as Ulysses S. Grant's home.

www.whitehouse.gov

Official Web site for the White House, the president's residence at 1600 Pennsylvania Avenue in Washington, D.C. Visitors can take a video tour of the White House, view photos of past and present first families, read presidential biographies, and check out the just-for-kids pages.

www.sidwell.edu

Web site for Sidwell Friends, the private school in Washington, D.C., attended by Malia Obama. Students can learn about the school's Quaker philosophy as well as its history and what fifth-grade students like Malia do in class.

page

2: Martin Schoeller/People/ASP

7: Bill Greenblatt/UPI Photo

10: Oliver Douliery/Abaca Press/MCT

13: David Katz/Obama for America/PRMS

15: Chuck Kennedy/MCT

16: Tannen Maury/EFE

17: Obama for America/PRMS

18: David Burnett/Contact Press Images

21: Obama for America/PRMS

22: Obama for America/PRMS

24: Obama for America/PRMS

26: Obama for America/PRMS

29: Obama for America/PRMS

30: John Lee/Chicago Tribune/MCT

32: Chicago Tribune/MCT

34: Obama for America/PRMS

37: Obama for America/PRMS

39: Paris Match/NMI

41: Obama for America/PRMS

42: Obama for America/PRMS

44: Chris Carlson/AP Photo

46: Rick Wilking/Reuters

48: Gus Ruelas/AP Photo

51: Talk Radio News/PRMS

52: Obama for America/PRMS

55: Alex Brandon/AP Photo

56: People Magazine/NMI

Front cover: Paul J. Richards/AFP Photo

ABOUT THE AUTHOR

Gail Snyder is a freelance writer and advertising copywriter who has written more than ten books for young readers. She lives in Chalfont, Pennsylvania, with her husband, Hal, and daughter Ashley.